Pottery for Juniors

Harold Powell

LONDON

BLANDFORD PRESS

ISBN 07137 0541 8

To
Andrew and Janet Greenwood

Typeset by H. Charlesworth & Co. Ltd., Huddersfield
Printed by Fletcher & Son Ltd, Norwich
Colour plates printed by Jarrold & Sons Ltd, Norwich
Bound by Richard Clay (The Chaucer Press) Ltd, Bungay

Contents

666

P

9898

Preface

Following upon the successful publication of my five previous books on pottery, and the many enquiries and letters received, it has become evident that the time is ripe for a book addressed to juniors. So many junior schools now possess kilns, and so many teachers are keen to experiment with their classes, that a book on the junior approach is essential. Only simple skills are necessary both for those teaching at this level and also for the children themselves.

In the first part of the book, which is addressed to the children, I have outlined in simple steps, and with photographs, a number of pottery making processes which I know can be attempted successfully. It forms a kind of 'pottery picture book' with many of the instructions given in the captions and complete explanations of the processes at the beginning of each chapter. The photographs feature two of my students, Andrew and Janet Greenwood, and I would like to express my appreciation to them, and to their parents for their ready co-operation. At the time of writing this book I was teaching at Marple Hall Grammar School for Boys and I am grateful to the Headmaster and Governors for their help.

In order that no process shall appear complicated, I have covered all the technical skills involved in the second part of the book which is more particularly addressed to the teachers. From the requests, and on the advice of many teachers, I have tried to meet the need of those in primary schools who have to teach academic subjects as well as art and crafts, in which they may not specialise, for a practical book of clear instruction and information will save them many hours in reading up technical manuals or attending lengthy courses. Approximate metric equivalents are given for all measurements used in the book.

Many of the 'tips' I have given have come from my own unique experience over twenty years of teaching infant, junior, secondary modern, grammar and art school students, and from the lectures given to teachers. The additional experience of teaching spastic children and of training their teachers has been a particularly rich one and given me great satisfaction. The setting up of craftrooms and workshops for them and for mentally handicapped students has been most worthwhile. Many of the teachers in these ventures had no pottery training beyond the short courses I have been able to provide, and here I would put in a plea to those practising the craft - wherever there are spastic schools in your area, be generous and offer your help and expertise to introduce pottery to these children. My own experience convinces me that the head teachers would be delighted, and you would be richly rewarded for your efforts.

Pottery is an old craft, and admitted by educationalists as one of the most rewarding in the training it provides and the excellent results obtained. It gives an instant stimulus to which students and teachers respond with unbounded enthusiasm. I hope that this book will convince many that it is a craft which may be extended successfully into far more junior schools, providing the children with an exciting interest and creating extremely pleasing results.

1   May we come in? Andrew and Janet have come to make some pots.

Introduction

You are sure to know that pottery is made from clay and baked but before you start, we need to take a closer look at the simple processes which are involved in making pottery. When you have read this introduction, you can take a look at the first section and find out how to make some exciting pots like Janet and Andrew have made. In the second section there are more details about the materials you will need and some additional information. This part is particularly for teachers, who will be able to give you more help. At the end of the book is a glossary which explains some of the unusual words used by potters, which you will find in the book, and you can use this like a dictionary.

When you start making your pots, you will need clay but, before you can make it into anything, you will need to prepare it. Within your lump of clay you may find parts that are not well mixed or which contain pockets of air and first you will need to knock the air out of it or else, when you bake your pot, the air which is still trapped in the clay will explode and blow your pot to pieces. This preparation of the clay is called 'wedging' and in picture 17 you can see Andrew has been doing this. You will have to do this with every piece of clay you use, and, even if it takes you quite a long time, it is worth it to ensure that your pot does not blow up when it is fired.

When you have made the pot in whichever way you choose, you will have to bake it. This is called firing and is done by putting all the pots into a large type of oven called a kiln. The kiln is sealed shut and the heat is turned on. During the firing time the kiln reaches a very high temperature and the pots must stay in the sealed kiln for a long period.

It may take as long as a day to cool down again before you can take the pots out. This first firing is called the 'biscuit' firing and, by this time, your pots will be as hard as stone and you will not be able to alter their shape.

At this stage they will be very plain and will be a pale brown, white or dull red colour, depending on the type of clay you have used, so the next thing to do is to colour them with a glaze. There are many exciting ways of decorating pots, which I will describe later in the book. Glaze is a liquid and, before it is fired, it looks like paint; indeed, you coat your pot with it as if it were paint. Then you fire it in the kiln and, when it comes out, you will see that it has become shiny, for glaze is in fact a kind of glass coat. You will then have an exciting pot and I am sure that now you will want to begin.

6

SECTION ONE: POTS FOR YOU TO MAKE AND DECORATE

1 How to dig and prepare the clay

'Can we make pots from our garden clay?' Andrew asked me this question, and it is one which is asked by many children and adults.

The answer of course is 'Yes' but the quality of the clay will depend on many things. For instance, where you live, if you have a garden, and a host of other things, which I will deal with later.

2   Starting to dig

---

3   Andrew has reached the clay.

This picture is taken in my garden and there you see Andrew digging through the soil to reach the clay, not very far down, as you can see.

Just about 10 inches (25.4 cm) below the soil, Andrew is already cutting slices of clay. It is a yellowish clay but streaked with darker colours.

4 We are trying to select the cleanest pieces.

5 Andrew has made his choice, but Janet isn't sure.

'Will this make pots?' Andrew asks. Janet thinks it is a bit messy, and dirty, and there are small stones in it too. Yes, it will make pots but we shall have to clean it first.

Andrew's second question is 'How can you clean clay?' Well, we shall dry the clay by keeping it in a warm place. In summer-time we may leave it in the sun. When the weather is damp, we need to bring it indoors.

Andrew and Janet have spent many hours in my studio, and have seen me making pots on the wheel. They too have made pots and we have had some exciting times when the finished, glazed models have come out of the kiln. Not all their pots survived the first firing which we call the 'biscuit firing' but generally they have managed to rescue some for glazing. Potters call this second firing 'glost firing'.

The clay I use does not look much like the clay they are looking at in the picture, and they look a little doubtful as they handle these messy lumps. I suggest that they experiment with it later to see it if will make good pots. However, I have already dried a few pieces of garden clay and now we will prepare some so that we may get on with our potting.

8

6   The dry clay must be broken up into small pieces, and Janet
      enjoys using the hammer.

7   Andrew says the crushing of the clay into fine powder is an
      important task. He is looking for stones and any other matter
      which does not look like clay.

8   We put the powdered clay into a bucket, add water and stir. The stirring will take some time so it is a good idea to take it in turns for it is tiring work. A pint of water (0.6 litre) is needed for every pound (about 450 gm) of clay to make the right mixture.

9   When the mixture is a smooth liquid we are ready for the next process.

10   The liquid clay is poured into a bowl through a coarse sieve.
        You can see the number on the side, 60. This is a fairly coarse
        sieve but a 40, which is coarser, can be used instead.

---

11   Here you can see Andrew using a stiff brush to force the sticky
        liquid through the tiny holes. The proper name of this liquid
        is slip.

12   We found a few stones and a lot of coarse sand in the sieve. A potter would tell you many things about the clay by looking into the sieve. He would probably tell you that this clay would make good bricks if it contained a little less sand.

---

13   We have found a large container made from plaster-of-paris, and here you see us pouring the clay into it.

14   The slip clay must remain in the plaster mould for several hours before the excess water is absorbed by the plaster.

---

15   We are a little impatient and want to see if the slip is setting into a plastic clay which we can model, but it is still very wet and sticky on the top.

16   Our patience is now rewarded. We have waited six hours and now Andrew is ready to prepare the clay for modelling.

---

17   Andrew has been throwing the clay on to the concrete bench. We call this wedging. It presses all the air bubbles out of the clay, which would explode our pots in the kiln.

18   Janet is holding the lump of clay while Andrew slices through it with a thin wire. We are looking to see if all the air bubbles have gone.

---

19   There is just one left. Can you see it? Andrew will join the halves together and bang the clay on to the bench a few more times.

We have been looking at pictures showing how common garden clay might be prepared for making pots. As you will have noticed it is a long process and would involve a lot of time and trouble to prepare enough clay for use in the classroom. One must also remember that much of the clay in and around our gardens contains sand in large proportions, and that too much sand affects the modelling qualities of the clay.

However, digging clay from near your home is a good introduction to pottery making in school, because you can compare the colour and firing qualities of your clay with that which the clay merchant supplies. The clay dug in the garden will differ in colour according to where you live. Ours was located in Marple, near Manchester. All the clay for miles around fires much the same colour, that is, a light terra-cotta (light brown) colour, and much of it is suitable for making common bricks.

If we were to move further south into Cheshire the colour would change considerably. Instead of firing a light colour the clay would be much darker, and this is because it contains a larger amount of iron which stains the clay both in the raw and in the fired stages.

You could strengthen your clay, and make it easier to model if you collected some clay from the county of Dorset and mixed the two clays together. You would need to know the correct proportions, of course, and that is why for school or hobby potting it is best to buy your clay from the clay specialists so that your final results are not achieved so much by luck as by using tried and tested materials.

When you have mixed your clay into a liquid and brushed it through the sieve, you might examine the mixture of materials which have not passed through the mesh. If the clay has been cut just beneath the surface of the ground there may be pieces of pottery or cinders, and many other pieces of household refuse, reminding us of the people using this land perhaps a hundred years ago, or more, but if you get your clay from ground which has lain undisturbed it may only contain a few stones, and sometimes a lot of coarse sand. You should examine this residue for it might yield fossils and interesting rocks (see picture 12).

When the clay is hardening against the side of the plaster mould you will have the same problem which faces the industrial clay maker. The clay will remain softer in the middle and on the surface, so as soon as possible you must turn the clay over so that the soft parts may come into contact with the plaster (picture 15). When your clay is plastic enough to remove from the plaster mould, you should wedge the clay thoroughly. This means that you must throw the clay lump on to a firm table of wood, concrete or plaster, cutting it with a piece of wire occasionally to see if any air bubbles are trapped in the clay (pictures 16 to 19). When this is done you may start to plan your pottery making.

2 The stone wall pot

It has long been the practice of beginners making their first pots to start by making thumb and coil pots. Neither of these is easy for young hands to model. The pot shown in this chapter is by quite a different method which has given both young and older students encouragement in their attempts to gain success.

First prepare the clay, as already described.

Next mix the slip, sometimes known as potter's glue for it sticks together the clay pieces. The recipe is given below. When the pot is fired, the slip becomes pottery with the rest of the model.

As you follow these instructions, look carefully at the pictures 20 to 47 which will show you what to do.

First, roll a piece of clay about the size of an orange into a flat slab. Use the wooden guides to determine the thickness.

Cut the base with a tile cutter into a round or square shape (or it can be cut with a knife).

Pull off pieces of clay to roll into balls; try to keep them all the same size.

Form each clay ball into a stone as shown in pictures 23 to 27.

Paint the base which you have cut with the slip (liquid clay) so that it makes a ½ inch (1.3 cm) border.

Now begin to lay the stones looking at the pictures to see how this is done. The end of each stone must be painted with slip and then pushed firmly against the one it is touching. Note the position of the first stone on the second row (31). It crosses the joint of the two bottom corner stones. When you have reached the height you want, press a board lightly on top of the pot. The pot will look better if the stone shapes are not smoothed off, so do not be tempted to smooth the outside of the finished pot. You will appreciate this point when the pot is glazed. The instructions for glazing are given later. Making a round pot is illustrated in pictures 34 to 38. Notice how Janet makes a lid (39 to 45).

Making the slip

If you are making your pot with brown clay, then of course the slip must be made from the same clay. The easiest way to mix it quickly is by using brown clay powder rather than the modelling clay. You could use some pieces of dry clay and powder it by crushing it with a rolling pin, mix it thoroughly with water so that it can be poured and it is then ready for use.

A tile cutter.

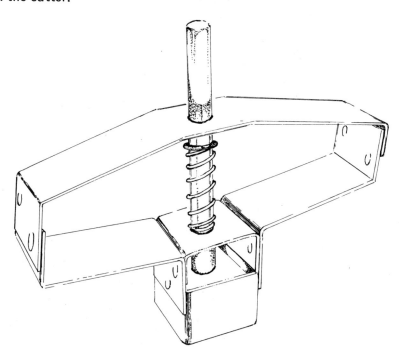

20   Rolling a slab of clay between wooden guides.

---

21   Cutting square and round shapes to make bases for pots.

22   Pulling off pieces of soft clay.

23   Rolling balls, all the same size. These will be formed into 'stones' for building up the pot.

24   Hold between finger and thumb and squeeze.

---

25   Pressing with finger and thumb of other hand.

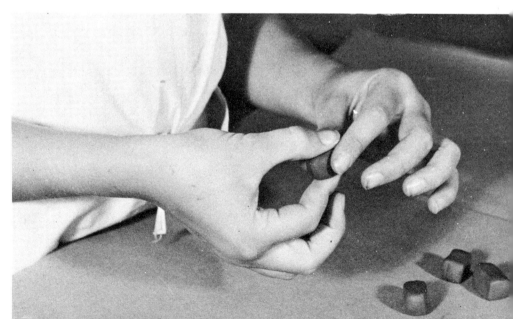

26   Turn the shape to flatten the ends.

---

27   Paint the tile edge with liquid clay.

28   Laying the stones. Paint the end of each stone with liquid clay and press firmly together.

---

29   Turn the end brick to start the second side.

30   Cutting the last stone to fit into the space.

---

31   Paint a layer of liquid clay over the stones, and lay the first
            stone of the second layer as shown.

32   Here Andrew puts in the last stone. Janet has watched so she
      will know how to make her pot.

---

33   Janet cuts a circular base.

34 Janet paints round the edge with liquid clay. She has already made some stones to place in position.

35 Here Janet is being shown how to bend the stone slightly to make it fit the circular shape.

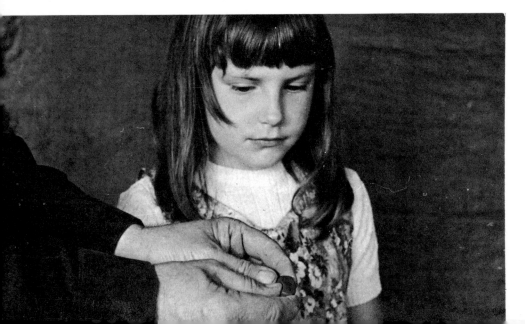

36   Now she places her first stone.

---

37   The last stone is cut to fit into the space.

38 Janet places the last stone in position.

---

39 Janet cuts two circular shapes for the lid. The smaller one is to be stuck on to the larger one with slip. It is important that the smaller one fits easily into the pot.

40   Again paint with liquid clay where the small tile must fit.

---

41   Ready to place.

42   Press and slide into position.

---

43   Try on for size.

44   Now make a knob.

---

45   Does the lid fit?

46   Painting the pots with tin-glaze.

---

47   Applying the coloured glazes.

3 Stone wall pot with coloured slip decoration

Now that you have mastered the art of making regular shapes with your clay stones, you may use your skill to make another attractive pot.

Look at pictures 48 to 56.

First, roll out the slab of clay.

Draw a rounded shape on a piece of paper, and then cut it out with a pair of scissors. Let the shape be of your own choosing, bearing in mind a possible use for the model. It could be used as an ornament or for holding flowers. An oval is a good shape to choose.

Lay the paper shape on the slab and cut round it carefully with a pointed knife.

The rules of building are just the same as with your first pot, but if you like you may choose to vary the shapes of your stones, if you are clever enough to keep the rim of the pot level when you reach the top layer. Or you may even leave the top layer uneven as you might if you were building one of our real old stone walls.

The decoration is simple. Cover the bottom of the pot with a layer of white slip-clay. Then, using the special dispensers, or, if these are not available, small teaspoons, trail lines of coloured slip across and on top of the white slip. By moving the pot (while it is still on the modelling board) and tilting it slightly, the coloured slips will form a marbled pattern on the base. You must remember to hold the pot on the board while performing this operation, otherwise the pot will finish as a sticky mess on the floor. Do not move the slips around for too long or they will all mix together and the result will be rather disappointing. When the pot has been fired to biscuit stage, it is then covered with a transparent glaze and fired again.

You will find the recipe for making the coloured slip on the next page.

Making the coloured slip

Liquid clays, usually white, are used as the base for your coloured slips. The amount of stain you use depends upon the intensity of the colour you desire. The amounts the manufacturer recommends will vary between 10 and 15 per cent of powder stain. In time, and with practice you will be able to judge the amount of stain to use by the colour of the clay stain mixture.

There is an exception to this. Some potters use raw colours such as copper and cobalt oxides. These are much stronger than the prepared stains, and not so much is required to colour the slip, but practice mixings need to be made with oxide stains for although copper produces green, and cobalt blue, the oxides are black before they are fired and therefore give no indication of the shades of colour they will give when fired. Prepared clay stains would be safer to use so that the true colour may be determined from the colour of the powder.

---

48   Janet rolls the slab of clay, and Andrew cuts a paper shape.

49   Janet cuts round the paper shape.

50   The pot is almost finished.

51   Andrew pours white slip into the clay shape, covering the base.

---

52   The excess slip is poured out.

53   Now Janet trails lines of coloured liquid clay. The colours are green, black, pink and yellow.

54   Andrew swirls the colours around the model to make a marbled pattern.

55   The pot has been fired, and is now about to be given a coating of transparent glaze.

---

56   Janet counts two seconds while the pot is fully immersed, and then removes it from the bowl of transparent glaze.

4 Making pots from natural shapes

In industry and most school pottery classes plaster moulds are used to form pottery models. The mould is used to support and shape the slab clay. Some of these plaster moulds are called 'mushroom' moulds, because the thin clay slab is placed on top of a convex shape and the excess clay is trimmed off. Often a clay foot is fastened to the base, and when the model is hard enough it is removed from the mushroom mould and finally smoothed, ready for firing.

This is work for older students who are probably more used to handling plaster-of-paris. But there are other objects ready made for us which we can use for supporting and shaping our pots, and it is more exciting when you collect these objects yourself. In picture 57, you can see Janet and Andrew looking at a collection of large stone shapes. They were found by a river bank. Wherever you live, and especially near the sea, there will be some stones to be found, and you should collect those which have large flat areas and pleasant curves.

Now to make the first pot from the stone you have chosen. Again you must roll a slab of clay. Judge the amount of clay you think necessary to cover the stone, and then either drop the clay on to the stone, or if you are nervous about your aim, just place and press the clay in position. You must avoid pressing the clay too far over the stone, or it will not come away when dry. In fact, in drying the clay will crack badly as it tries to shrink away from the stone. Mark a line around the clay with a pencil and cut it away (picture 63).

You may place three legs in position to form the base, or if the stone is fairly regular shape you might make a foot from a coil of clay (see picture 81). Stick them firmly into position with slip (picture 64).

Wait until the clay is stiff before removing it from the stone. Most stones have a porous quality so the clay model should be easy to remove.

Finally, rub a wet finger or damp sponge along the final cut so that the edge of the model will not crack (picture 65).

57   We look at the stones.

---

58   We choose those which we like best.

59   The rolled slab is held in position over the stone, and dropped on to it.

---

60   This one is not successful, try again.

61   Better luck this time.

---

62   Andrew presses the clay over the stone.

63   Now he cuts on a marked line with a craft knife.

---

64   The children are sticking legs on the base with slip. They must be careful to position them correctly.

65 The models are now 'soap hard' and the children are smoothing the edges with damp sponges.

---

66 This is one way to decorate the pot. Drop spots of tin glaze on to a background glaze.

5 The leaf pot

The leaves you see illustrated were collected in May when they were soft and easy to press into the clay. It does not really matter when you collect the leaves except, of course, in late autumn or winter.

We are using sycamore and horse-chestnut leaves, and find sycamore are better. There are sycamore trees in many parts of England, and many similar trees all over the world.

Wherever you live you can usually find suitable leaves with which to make your pots. You need large leaves, of course, to make large dishes. The making of the shapes is simple, although you may be surprised to see that instead of knives the children are using needles. The needle is pressed with a quick stabbing movement around the fine points of the leaf.

When this is completed the leaf is removed immediately, the edges of the clay shape are gently raised to give the shape a curved look. In the case of the sycamore each pointed section of the leaf is curved separately.

There are many ways of decorating the leaf shapes. Generally in junior schools it is sufficient to dip the model into a coloured glaze. Where the vein marks are deepest the coloured glaze will be darkest, and this makes a most pleasing contrast with the smoother parts of the pot. One can, of course, experiment with various coloured glazes.

With the help of your teacher you could cut a piece of thin paper the same shape as the leaf but much smaller or you might use a smaller leaf to make it easier. With a little cold-water paste stick the paper shape in the centre of the fired pot. Then dip the pot in a background glaze, and when the glaze is dry (usually within a few seconds) remove the paper shape. You can now choose a glaze of a different colour and paint it in the centre shape left by the paper mask.

There is a lovely new red glaze available now which would be very attractive in the centre of the leaf shape.

Instructions for firing

1 Use white or buff clay.

2 Fire at the temperature recommended by the supplier, or a little lower.

3 Test the fired pot whilst at the biscuit stage by touching it with the tip of your tongue. If your tongue sticks to the pot, then the glaze mixing must be thin. This means adding more water.

67   Pricking out the leaf.

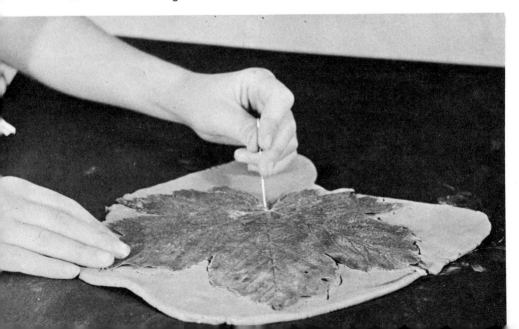

68   Turning up the edges.

---

69   The leaf shape has been fired, and is now ready to be decorated. Andrew is holding the pot over the bowl of coloured glaze.

COPPER GRE
TRANS.

70   The fired leaf dipped in green glaze.

---

71   This leaf has been biscuit fired and a paper mask fastened to it with cold water paste.

72   Dipping the model into a background glaze.

73   The paper leaf has been removed and Andrew is now painting
the space with a glaze of contrasting colour.

6 Fish tank arches

So many of you have fish tanks or bowls at home or at school, that it seems a good idea to make the special arches, bridges and rockery which make the tanks so attractive.

Buying these in shops is expensive, whereas clay is cheap and even in a small kiln you can fire a large number in one firing.

It is not necessary to glaze your arches, because the absorbent biscuit pottery will soon become green with tiny plants which grow in the tank. Indeed it would not be wise to use pottery colours on the models for they could have a harmful effect upon some of your fish. Copper colourants and lead glazes might in time contaminate the water sufficiently to kill the fish.

There are some 'do's and don'ts' to observe. First, the clay should be smoothed so that there are not too many sharp corners. If you are making a rockery-type arch for a small bowl, make sure that the holes are fairly large so that your fish may pass through easily.

If you use the technique of making clay weeds to stick to the arch, it is a good idea to press the top of the sieved clay gently, to prevent the clay firing with sharp edges. I am told by an expert on tropical fish that the fish only rub themselves against the rocks when they are suffering from some ailment, and in their natural habitat they would certainly meet sharp rocks, so perhaps these precautions may sound too alarming; however, it is better to be sure that the fish will not suffer any injury.

For the large tank the type illustrated in the picture is obviously the best. Andrew has made a fairly thick slab of clay with which to support the coil arches. This is the thickest piece, and must be wedged thoroughly to make sure there are no air bubbles left inside. You may decorate the long coils of clay before looping them over the centre support. Either a simple thumb press or an incised marking is sufficient.

If a long coil crosses the centre support it must be modelled into position. This means pulling the clay from the coil into the large supporting piece, making a perfect joint. It is not enough just to stick the clay. While the clay is soft it will appear to adhere to the support, but on drying you will find that the two pieces have shrunk away from each other. The same rule applies if you fasten a short piece to the centre or to one of the large coils. Simple adhesion is not enough, the pieces must be modelled together. A little clay slip between the two joints is always a good thing and will ensure a safe firing.

The second arch is a simple bridge shape (78). Make a nicely shaped arch wide enough to span the bottom of your bowl, then if you place a pile of small stones in the bottom of the bowl it will become far more interesting both for the fish and for you.

Some children like to start modelling with a solid piece of clay (77). This they press into shape, and then push their thumbs through to form several holes through which the fish can swim.

Remember these simple rules

1 Thick clay to be wedged thoroughly.
2 Good adhesion by modelling and perhaps the use of clay slip.
3 Good shapes, and large holes in the rockery model.

Making weed or plant growth is fascinating, so much so that some children will go on making it until there is enough to fill the tank. The secret is to use it sparingly, and this means making it sparingly.

A domestic flour sieve will give the best results. It is possible of course to use a pottery sieve and it will make a fine silky strand, but continuous use will strain and eventually break the fine mesh of the sieve. Before scraping the sieved clay, paint a little clay-slip where it is to be placed. This will make doubly sure that the fine strands will fire on successfully.

Finally, do not fire the models at too high a temperature. Terra cotta about 1020 to 1040 °C will leave the biscuit model absorbent enough for the plants to adhere. Buff or grogged clays may be fired at a much higher temperature, probably up to 1100 °C.

---

74 Making a large arch for the big tank. Here Andrew is fitting the arches to the centre piece. The centre is very thick as you can see.

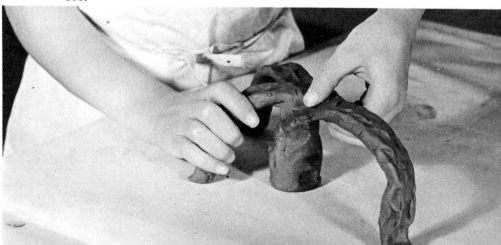

75   Weeds and plants made from clay are added.

---

76   The large arch completed.

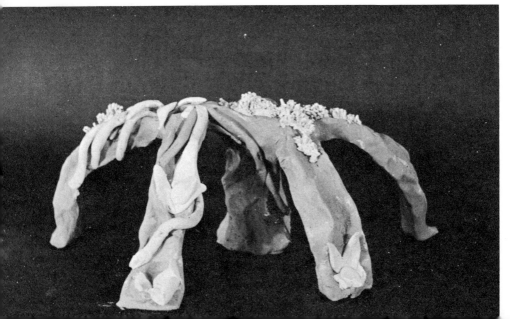

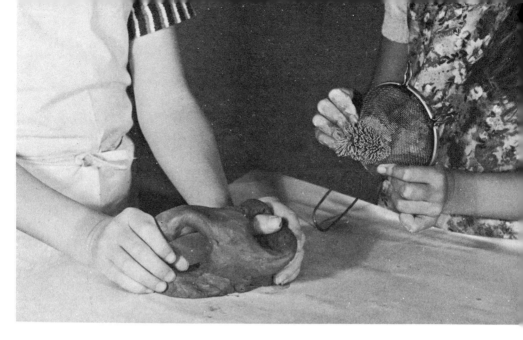

77   Andrew models the rockery. Janet sieves the clay.

---

78   Here is a simple bridge-shaped arch for a bowl. Clay is pushed through a sieve and scraped off to decorate the arch.

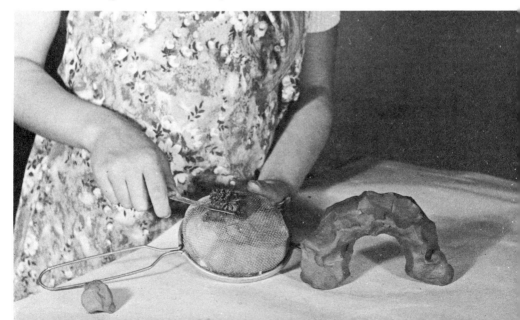

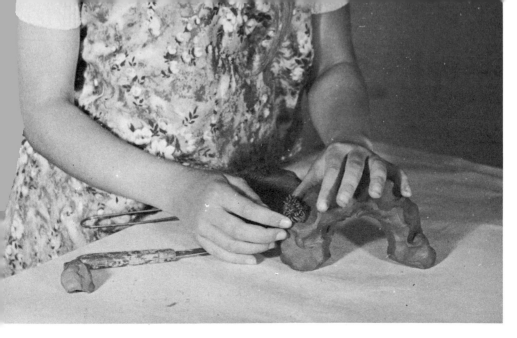

79   Placing the 'plant' in position.

---

80   Putting the fired arch into the fish bowl.

7 Fun animals

The animal models in the next few pages are intended to stimulate rather than lay down a pattern for making models. When modelling with clay which is to be fired and decorated it is essential for certain rules to be followed. For instance, arms and legs made with soft clay will adhere immediately to the body of the figure being modelled, but on drying the pieces will shrink and almost certainly fall away. So, when making figures, it is necessary to join the limbs in position by 'modelling' in the same way that a perfect joint was achieved when making the fish tank arches. By using this technique the figure is made into a 'solid piece', and sometimes, for extra safety, a fillet of clay can be pressed between two parts of the figure to give it extra support.

You will notice that because Andrew has cut the tail of the seal he must model a piece of clay at the end of the cut so that the sharp cut will not extend further and crack the model when it dries (87).

Sometimes rubbing a wet finger between joints, thereby creating slip on the surface, will be sufficient to seal a joint. And of course liquid clay which you know as slip, and which has already been used to stick stones together, can often be used when sticking flat pieces together.

Making two-legged figures to stand is probably the most difficult task you will encounter. The simple way for you to do this is to cut out a shape as if you were making a gingerbread man, and start to model a standing figure from this shape. When you have made your basic shape of the human body, then you can dress the figure by the following method:

Roll some clay into a thin flat slab using rulers as rolling guides, then cut strips of clay in the shape of coats or dresses, or if your figure is a highwayman or a sailor, cut strips of this thin clay and press around the knee to represent high boots. Dressing figures with thin slabs of clay is exciting and you can make a host of historical or modern figures.

If you have difficulties in making the figure stand, then make a seat and bend the figure into a sitting position.

Animals can usually be made from one piece of clay when the limbs are pulled from the main body. Tortoises and rabbits are popular subjects and you should not find it too difficult to make these. It is a good idea to look at some drawings and cartoons of animals and figures. Notice how the artist often looks for a simple way of portraying the figures. Look also at the actual animals when you can, and notice the shape of their heads and bodies.

81 Janet is rolling a coil. Andrew is too but his will be a torpedo shape.

---

82 Janet is making hers into a 'walking worm'.

83   The humps are modelled, now for the tail.

---

84   Here is the little figure ready for firing.

85   Andrew has chosen a more difficult figure to model. He is making a seal. He cuts the narrow end to make the tail.

---

86   He opens the cut, and models the tail by twisting and smoothing.

87   A small coil of clay is pressed into the opening to prevent cracking.

---

88   The seal is now resting on a rock. The rock is formed by inverting a thumb pot. Therefore the rock is not solid. Andrew has made the flippers, and is modelling them to the body.

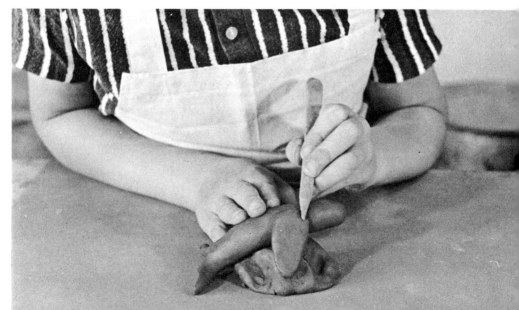

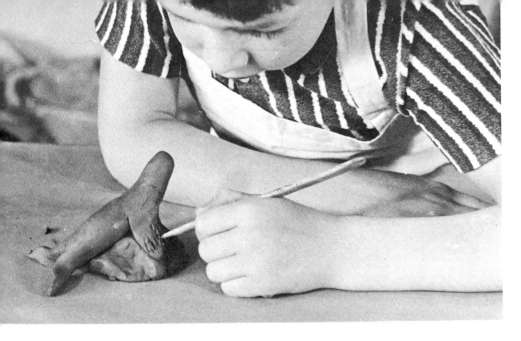

89   The seal's head is raised, and Andrew is putting the finishing touches to the flippers.

---

90   Andrew has made a model from polystyrene ceiling tiles. He has fastened pieces of broken tile with special adhesive, and is covering the shapes with plaster.

91   Andrew's project completed.

92   Janet has made a model and is now painting it. It is a background for some model rabbits.

8 First models

Even very small children can make simple models and pots. Here you see Sarah making some.

| 93 | Janet rolls a ball of clay for Sarah to press. | 94 | Janet presses Sarah's fingers into the clay. |

95   Sarah paints one of her pots. Notice her collection of finished 'shells', and 'Mummy with baby' model.

96   Here Sarah shows her clay 'shells'. You can also see some thumb pots which she has made and these have been glazed.

9 Tiles

There are many ways of making tiles and some methods are quite simple. There are simple ways also of assembling the tiles to make table mats and small tables which junior children might attempt.

Your clay must be rolled between wooden rolling guides so that it is of a standard thickness. White clay would be best to use since it would provide a good background on which to use the many beautiful pottery colours. The rolled clay must be left in a warm place for some time so that it becomes stiff. You can assist this by placing the slabs on top of a warm kiln, but, this means constantly checking to see that the clay does not become too hard to cut. Do not cut the tiles while the clay is soft or they will distort when they are handled.

Cutting the tiles (Picture 97)

This stiff condition is known to potters as 'leather hard', although a usual definition used in schools is 'soap hard'. It is possible to cut the tiles with a knife using a ruler and working very carefully. The best and most effective way is to use a tile cutter. The one you see illustrated on page 18 is one and an eighth inch (2.8 cm) square cutter, and there are many other sizes. If you have any difficulty in obtaining these cutters you should write to me and I will arrange for supplies to be sent to you.

This small cutter produces a tile when fired of one inch (2.5 cm) square, and this is a good size when planning the models you intend to make. When the tiles are cut and dry they may be stacked in piles of six or over. Being small they will dry without the risk of warpage. The biscuit firing should not be too high so that the tiles will remain porous, and will pick up the coloured glazes, giving a coating thick enough to ensure a complete covering and even distribution of the coloured glaze.

Arranging the tiles (Picture 99)

The illustrations 99 to 101 show how the tiles are spaced and grouted. This is simply a matter of pouring plaster-of-paris between the tiles. The grouting is not absolutely necessary, the tiles could be placed close together, but the white divisions between the tiles frame them and make them more distinctive. You will probably enjoy making and glazing these small tiles for table mats and small tables and trays. Probably the most attractive way of arranging the coloured tiles is in what we term 'random' fashion. After selecting the colours you like, start to lay the tiles on to a piece of plywood or chipboard. Lay two of one colour; one of another, repeat the first colour, lay two or three of a third colour, insert one of very distinctive shade, say black, or white. Continue to do this until a random sort of pattern emerges. After a lot of practice you will get used to laying patterns which are not geometrical, but which through the dominance of certain colours give a distinctive colour pattern.

Grouting   (Pictures 100 and 101)

The pictures show clearly how the grouting of tiles is accomplished. First, though, if plaster is to be used it must be mixed correctly. Mix in small amounts so that there is never any hard plaster left in the bowl. Pour a third of a cup of cold water into the bowl, add by sprinkling, the plaster-of-paris, and when all the water is absorbed stir the mixture and pour over the tile mat or table. Pour at the top edge and with a kidney rubber or a piece of cardboard scrape the wet plaster to the bottom. You may have to mix several bowls of plaster, but this is safer than having a large mix which dries before it is used up. Scrape as cleanly as possible, and finally clean with a cloth and polish with a piece of news-paper.

Making a textured pattern   (Pictures 102 to 104)

Textured tiles can be made by several methods. Tree bark produces attractive tiles, and these may be varied by the different textures of bark on the tree branches. The tree branch need not be thick since it is the bark shape we require. Make sure that you cut a fairly true cylinder, with interesting bark textures. Roll the clay between rolling guides, remove the sticks and then roll the tree branch firmly along the length of the slab. Obviously only one movement is required otherwise the texture pattern will be spoiled.

You may also glue pieces of felt on to your rolling pins, make patterns of string and rice on them, roll them in wet plaster, and in fact use any material you think might produce pleasing textures.

A sure success is to empty your pockets, and search for keys and other items which you might press into the clay. Do not aim for a geometrical design, but use the items to press areas of pattern over the tile. With all these textured designs the best type of decoration, and the most effective, is a simple covering of coloured transparent glaze. The glaze lies thicker in the depressions caused by the pressing, and the difference in colour shade produces a dramatic decoration.

Remember these simple rules

The techniques to remember are as follows: when making tiles which are to be decorated with glaze, underglaze colour or crayon, the clay must dry to 'soap hard' condition before cutting. When making textured tiles the clay must be in its natural soft condition; if the tiles are large they must be lightly weighted to prevent distortion. A good idea is to weight the large tiles during the biscuit firing. You may fire a stack of six tiles and cover with a piece of half inch (1.3 cm) kiln bat. It is possible to buy small off cuts of kiln bats (shelves) for this purpose.

97   Cutting the small tiles.

98   Dipping the tiles into glaze after their first firing.

---

99   Placing with card spacers. (You can make these by cutting
          pieces of thin card.)

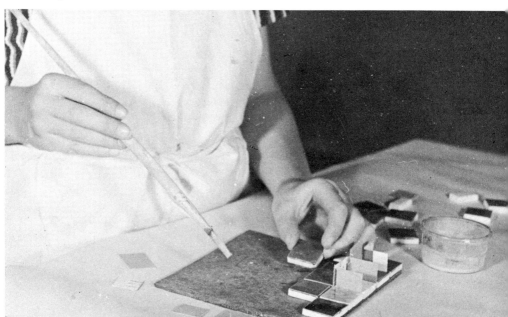

100   Applying the plaster.

101   Grouting the tile spaces.

102   Texturing soft clay with a piece of tree branch.

---

103   Janet is pressing scissor handles into the clay to make patterns.
           Note the glazed tile on the right.

104 Andrew is using various implements to press a design. Note the mark made by the tile cutter. This is a guide mark since pressing will alter the shape, the tile is not cut until the clay is soap hard.

105 Decorating a white tile with underglaze crayons.

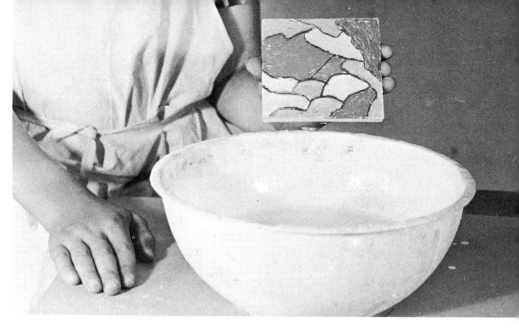

106   Ready for dipping into transparent glaze.

---

107   The colour is now covered with a transparent glaze, and ready for the glost firing.

10 Coil pots

No scheme of pottery making would be complete without the skills of coil making being included. There are several ways of making coil pots, some with the emphasis on safety, and some with speed of completion in mind. It is possible to meet both these requirements. The illustrations 109 to 114 show the construction and decorating processes.

Continuous coiling

This is the fastest method. When the base has been cut the clay coils are rolled, and you should make them as long as you can. The skill of coiling takes some time to acquire, so it is advisable to have some practice in trying to roll the coils evenly. The end of a coil should be pointed—and with the rolling action, it will usually go into a point at the end.

Paint around the base with slip-clay, and lay the coil around the edge. When you reach the starting point of the coil, take the rest of the clay up and over the top. Press it slightly into the point, and carry on with the coiling. Start the outside sealing process after laying this first coil. You can see in the picture 110 how Andrew is smoothing one coil into another. This of course seals the coil, and if some of the clay is left slightly raised it will give you a pleasing texture on which to use an opaque glaze. The problem with which you are faced when you reach the top is that it is not level. You can adjust this by rolling a short coil, thick in the middle and thin at each end, and place this in position to compensate for the hollow which has been present during the coiling of the pot.

Once the pot is level, and the sides smooth there will be no sign of the spiral rise of the long coils of clay. To make the top of the pot absolutely level you could rub it on a slate dampened with water, or if you have a wheel your teacher could cut a slice from the top with a needle.

Single coils

This is the safest method. In this process you cut a base, paint it with slip, and make and fix each coil separately. The ends of the coils are cut at an angle so that when they are placed together and painted with slip they will stick without showing the joint. There are two ways of sealing the coils, and one as you can see in the picture 113 incorporates the decoration of the pot. We call this incise decoration, when the coils are incised into each other with a modelling stick, or even using the end of a paint brush.

If you wish to leave the coil shape visible, then you must seal the inside coils with your thumb as the pot rises. You can decorate the outside by trailing coloured slips down the side of the pot as you see Andrew is doing in the photograph (114). As you progress coil pots will probably become the most important pots you will make.

In the senior schools pots of all shapes and sizes, and for all purposes, are made from coiling clay, and in fact this type of modelling would be included in most of the examinations set for senior students. You will make small models at first, but with practice very soon you will be making coil pots in all shapes and sizes, and with beautiful glaze decoration.

108 Here are some coil pots made by older children. The table lamp on the left was made by a senior boy. It was made by the continuous method and is 15 inches (40 cm) high.

109   Andrew is starting to build on the base with a long coil.

---

110   Here, he is sealing the coils on the outside of the pot.

111   He is adding a second coil. Look at the way he builds it in spiral fashion.

---

112   The spiral or continuous coiling leaves the pot uneven at the top. Andrew has shaped a coil to make the top level.

113 Andrew's first pot is on the right of the picture. The pot he is decorating has been built with single coils. Note the finished incised decoration on the third pot.

---

114 Another pot built with single coils. This time Andrew is trailing coloured slip down the side.

11 How to use your pottery kiln

Clay must be fired to a very high temperature to make it into pottery. This is a statement that all potters understand, and which must be understood by all students who want to make pots. A very high temperature would mean at least 1000 °C and that, compared with the heat of an electric cooker, is really quite high. When seen through the spy-hole of a pottery kiln the pots must be glowing red. When the colour is cherry red the temperature would probably be just below 1000 °C, so the colour we would be looking for would be a bright orange.

115   Staffordshire bottle kiln.

However, all school and hobby potters use some way of measuring the temperature so that the pots will be fired correctly. The two methods used are simple. The rather expensive pyrometer which gives a continuous reading is the better way of measuring because one can see at a glance what the temperature is, and calculate how long the firing will take. The other method is to put a special cone inside the kiln, opposite the spy-hole in the door. These cones are stamped with numbers which indicate at what temperature the cone will bend and when this temperature is reached the cone bends over completely. If the temperature is exceeded the cone will melt. This method is quite reliable, but of course it means lots of visits to the spy-hole when nearing the maturing temperature.

Most school kilns are heated by electricity, and the elements are inside the kiln looking almost like the elements in an electric fire. They are in fact almost the same. They may be thicker, and made from slightly different kinds of steel, but they work in a similar way.

Some kilns used in art schools and colleges are heated by gas. In this case the firing chamber or muffle is completely enclosed, and the gas jets send their heat around the muffle, which means that the muffle and the pots inside become red hot.

It is also possible to build a kiln which will burn coal or wood to heat the pots, and indeed there are still some 'bottle kilns' to be seen around the country which were once fired with coal. There are kilns still firing tiles and drain pipes where coal is used to heat up the kiln.

The bottle kiln produced some of the finest English china and earthenware in Europe. It had developed at a time when English creamware and later bone china was capturing the markets of Europe. In the illustration 115 you will see why the kiln got its name. It was fired by coal, through six or eight fire boxes situated around the outside. With continual stoking these kilns produced terrific heat. Of course since the fire and smoke filled the inside of the kiln, there had to be some way of protecting the white pottery otherwise it could not have been decorated with such beautiful colours. Fireclay boxes called saggars were made, the china and earthenware were placed inside, a lid was then placed on top and the filled saggars were stacked high in the bottle kiln. The entrance to the kiln was bricked up and then the fires were lit. Such was the heat that it might be three days before the kiln could be opened, and then the task of unloading was most uncomfortable for the workers. Some brick kilns today are heated by coal, and the sequence of firing each chamber containing hundreds of bricks can take five or six days.

There is evidence that the Romans in Britain contributed to the design of the bottle kiln. In the book *Kilns and Kiln Firing for the Craft Potter* by Harry Fraser (Pitman Press) there are some interesting sketches of early Roman kilns. From the simple earth kiln the Romans developed a kiln with several chambers heated by one fire. It is claimed that it required two tons (2000 kg) of wood to complete the firing and to reach the temperature necessary. From this a later kiln was made which had a pre-heating chamber. This must have been a useful development since it quickened the drying of the pots. This is in fact the principle of modern industrial firing. In modern pottery factories a moving truck filled with pottery passes slowly through a long tunnel kiln which is heated in the centre. As the trucks pass along the tunnel the temperature is rising, so that when the centre is reached the pots quickly reach the required temperature and slowly move towards the end of the tunnel where eventually the doors are opened to allow the truck to be unloaded.

The school or hobby kiln

The small modern electric kiln, which has almost transformed the teaching of art and craft in Great Britain, is a most efficient piece of equipment.

It is of course the most essential piece of equipment either for school or for the hobby potter. With this kiln one can produce craft pottery of the highest standard.

Maximum temperatures may be as high as 1300 °C although for junior pottery this temperature is not likely to be needed. Very little care or maintenance is required, and if the manufacturers' instructions are followed the kiln will fire for several years without attention. It is important to observe some simple precautions, and of course the teacher will always stack and unload the kiln. No doubt if you practise pottery at school you will be shown the stacked kiln, and also allowed to look inside the kiln after firing.

It is not likely that any educational authority will allow children of any age to operate the kiln, but it is possible that you will be able to observe the way in which a kiln is packed. One must fill it to capacity, and when firing clay models they may be placed on top of each other to use up all the space. Remember though that glazed pottery must not touch, or the pots will stick together.

Fireclay bats or shelves are used to build up the models in the kiln. They are rather brittle and should be handled with care. Props are used to build up the shelves, and these may be obtained in different sizes to accommodate pots of different heights. They are round supports which you can see at the front corner of the shelf in pictures 116 and 117.

It is essential that neither kiln shelves nor any of the pottery touch the elements. After a few firings the elements are covered with a powdery substance. This must not be disturbed, and therefore the elements should not be handled.

Then there are stilts. This is how they are described: a refractory support having three arms each terminating in an upward and downward point. These provide maximum support and minimum area of contact which is essential when firing glazed ware. Probably the illustration 117 and 118 will be self-explanatory. The stilt is made from high firing clay, the glazed pot sits on the three points of the stilt, and therefore the glaze, being molten at its highest temperature, will adhere only to the points and the pots will not stick to the kiln shelf.

Many potters clean off the glaze from the bottom of the pot and this helps to prevent accidents. If the glaze has been too thickly applied or the firing too high then the glaze could still run down the pot and stick on the shelf. So the golden rule is, clean off the base, and support the pot with a stilt.

116	Andrew is putting a stilt on the bat.	**117**	Now he places a pot on the stilt.

---

118   This is how the bats are built up. Note the unfired cone standing next to the one which has bent and melted in the kiln. We stand the cone in a small ball of clay. Note the stilts also.

The coloured illustrations

On the cover of this book, and on the following two pages you will see some coloured pictures of finished pots. Janet and Andrew have made all of these, except the rabbit figures, which were made by a friend, Mrs. Bellamy.

All the pots made by the children are described in this book, with instructions for making them.

The illustrations are as below:
On the cover:
top: Stonewall pots with slip decoration.
bottom: The rabbit scene. These rabbits were made by Mrs. Bellamy, and Janet made the background. You can see Janet making this on page 61.
On the following pages:
1. Stonewall pots, round and square. See pages 17 to 32 for instructions.
2. Pots made from natural shapes. See pages 39 to 44.
3. Fun animals, figures, and Sarah's first pots. See pages 55 to 63.
4. All shapes and sizes of tiles. These have been decorated in several ways, and you will find these methods described on pages 65 and 66.
5. Pots made from leaf shapes. See pages 45 to 49.
6. Coil pots of different shapes and sizes. See pages 72 to 76.

Note The materials used to make the pottery illustrated in this book were supplied by Messrs. Podmore and Sons Ltd., Caledonian Works, Shelton, Stoke-on-Trent, who also assisted with the chapter 8, Health Precautions.

Photographs by William A. Spilsbury

SECTION TWO: PRACTICAL SUGGESTIONS AND INFORMATION FOR THE TEACHER

1 The nature and care of clays and glazes

Although many students in the age range of nine to thirteen will be able to read and understand much of the information contained in the following pages, this section is mainly intended for teachers, and contains concise instructions and recommendations to help them with technical problems which will be met when starting pottery as a new craft. It should also provide helpful suggestions for those who wish to extend the scope of their pottery classes, and whose classroom facilities are limited.

About Clay

In the first section of the book we have been looking at pictures showing how common garden clay might be prepared for making pots. This is a good introduction to the craft of pottery, for it convinces children that garden clay is substantially the same kind as that supplied by the pottery merchant.

However, it is unlikely that any teacher, particularly those employed in junior schools, would have time to prepare local clay in the amounts which would be required to supply a class. Therefore once the experiment in clay preparation is completed and the children realise that the clay in the bin or the polythene bag is from the same source (the ground beneath us), you will have fewer difficulties and fewer broken pots if you use the clay which is specially prepared by experts for use in school. Below is a list of clays in general use.

Staffordshire Red

This is a dark brown clay which contains about 7% of iron. It fires to a rich terra cotta colour at $1040\,^\circ$C, and will fire a darker colour as the temperature is raised. It is an excellent clay for modelling, and the obvious choice for junior children. When the models are biscuit fired they may be covered with a white tin glaze, then over-painted with coloured glazes which produce remarkable results. The Staffordshire Red clay breaks through the tin-glaze in places, so that the combination of coloured glazes, and some of the tin-glaze merging together with the brown clay produces a beautiful coloured pattern. Potters refer to this clay as a 'kind' clay. This is because it has a high degree of plasticity, and is quickly and easily reconstituted.

White or Ivory Clay

Fired white clay has a drawing paper texture which forms an ideal background for underglaze painting. It is a difficult skill for young children and so a pottery crayon has been devised which even the youngest student can use. The crayons are made from pottery colours, so they show quite clearly beneath a transparent glaze.

There are simpler decorations which may be used whilst the clay is in its plastic state. One is known as slip decoration, when white clay in slip form may be stained with pottery colours and applied by brushing, trailing from a rubber bag through a glass tube, or simply by swirling the coloured slip around the base of a dish, making a marbled pattern.

Grogged clay

Many potters use grog in their clay. Grog is ground biscuit ware, usually produced by grinding broken tiles or reject pots which have not been glazed. The grog is added to give it strength, and to control the shrinkage. It also makes safer the firing of thick clay models.

There are different degrees of coarseness to suit the individual needs of the potter. However, without a machine known as a pug-mill it is difficult to introduce grog into the clay, so it is better to buy a clay which is ready grogged. The prepared grogged clay now available contains coarse sand as a grogging agent. The clay base is fireclay, and with the added sand the clay will fire to very high temperatures without the risk of distortion or cracking.

Garden clay

It is fun to use clay collected from local sources, and as previously mentioned collecting clay from different parts of the country would make an exciting project. It is not certain however that your glazes would always fire successfully with these clays so your main supply must come from the clay merchant whose glazes are made to match his clays.

Care of Clay

Clay is obviously the first thought of the potter. Whether in industry, school or the home, clay is the material with which we are most concerned. When the clay comes to you it will be carefully wrapped in polythene sheeting, or even completely enclosed in a polythene bag. This comparatively modern wrapping material has been a boon to the potter, ensuring that the clay arrives in excellent condition and remains soft and ready for use over a very long period. There will be times when perhaps a bag has split, and in a very short time the clay will go hard. So all consignments should be carefully examined and if a bag has become torn in transit the clay should immediately be covered with another polythene sheet.

The bags may be stored in a cool place until new clay is required, and if only a small amount has been used the bag may be resealed and put back into storage. Any scraps of clay left over, and which through contact with warm air have become a little stiff, should be stored in a clay bin. The best type of bin is the galvanised steel bin (or you may use a domestic dustbin). There should always be a spade available so that the clay scraps may be dampened and 'spaded'. It is almost certain that quantities of clay will build up in the bin over a period of potting, and it is essential that they are not wasted. If, when the lesson is over, helpers are chosen to clear away the scraps, they should chop the clay with the spade, sprinkle a little water over, and chop again. Then this chopped clay should be completely covered with a piece of polythene sheet. If you wish to use the clay next day it will be in perfect condition, and with a short period of 'wedging' will be ready for use once again.

You will soon discover that there are two other hazards which are certain to affect you. The first and most frustrating is when a large piece of clay has somehow been left uncovered for a short time and is too hard for modelling, and also too hard to chop and spade. The method of reconstituting this clay takes a fairly long time but it is always successful. You need a small galvanised bath, and strangely enough there always seem to be one or two available. Place two or three bricks in the bottom of the bath, put the clay on top of the bricks, and fill the bath with water, but only up to the level of the bricks (this is important). Find an old hessian sack and place it over the clay, making sure that it makes contact with the whole area. The sack will absorb the water and pass it on to the clay. You must check every day to see that water is kept at the brick level, and in a few days' time you will find that the clay has softened and is usable again. Do not be tempted to cover the clay completely with water; this would result in the clay dissolving into a messy slip if left for a long period, and make it quite unfit to model.

If, as sometimes happens, clay is left until it has become absolutely dry, or some of your models have broken before you have a chance to fire them, then you may keep some of the hard, dry clay with which to make slip. When the clay is broken into small pieces and rolled into dust with a rolling pin it will mix quite easily with water and when passed through a sieve will be ready for many uses in pottery making. If the hard clay pieces pile up and become unmanageable you may reconstitute the whole stock. Simply crush into small lumps, put into a bin and cover with water. The water should not be above the level of the clay. Leave until the water has saturated the clay, and then start the spading process. If the clay mass is too soft to use, then you could place several pounds of the sloppy clay between plaster bats. The plaster bats are obtainable from the clay merchant, or you could make them quite easily. All you need is a wooden frame, mix a bowl of plaster-of-paris and pour into the frame.

Small amounts of clay which have been left on the desk and become rather stiff, can be softened by 'pancaking'. As the word suggests you merely flatten the clay into a pancake, sprinkle a little water on to the surface, and then fold the outside edges over and press the water into the clay. Unless you are careful the water could squirt out into your face so make sure that water is sealed inside the clay.

Clay, Glaze and Colour

The first section of the book dealt with the methods used to make a selection of pots which should interest the junior student. This chapter is devoted to the materials used both in the making and the decoration of these pots. Each model is described separately so that once your models are biscuit fired you may consult these pages for instructions and suggestions for decoration. Glaze plays a major part in most of the decorative processes because the possibilities are so varied when stains and oxides are used to add colour to your pots, and when the best use is made of opaque and matt glazes. Most young children are puzzled by the effect of glaze upon their pots, and questions are often asked such as, 'Are we varnishing our pots?' and 'What is glaze?' You will find the answers to these questions in several technical books. A fairly simple definition is given in my last book *The Pottery Handbook of Clay, Glaze and Colour*, and for extra reading on the subject of pottery making it would make a useful addition to the teachers' library.

What is Glaze?

Glaze is glass; that is, in most cases it looks like glass, and one of the main constituents is silica from which glass is made. Add to the glass a flux such as lead or borax, and we have the beginnings of a transparent glaze. The manufacturers add other materials to produce different types of glazes, and to harden them so that they do not run down the pots when subjected to great heat. They also fit their glazes to the clays they produce. The word 'fit' has an important pottery meaning. The glaze manufacturers, when mixing their materials, must be aware of the behaviour of the clay when fired at high temperatures. There is further shrinkage of the pot whilst it is in the kiln, even when all the moisture appears to have left the clay, so this means a compensating shrinkage in the glaze to avoid the many glaze faults which can occur. This is the reason why most potters depend upon one source for their supplies.

2 A guide to the materials used in Section One

THE STONE WALL POT

Materials and equipment

Clay: Staffordshire Red
Tin glaze
Transparent glaze
Glaze stains either oxides or
prepared stains

Rolling pins
Rolling guides
Tile cutters

The stone wall pot has been fired at a temperature between $1040\,^{\circ}C$ and $1050\,^{\circ}C$, so the biscuit pot should be sufficiently porous to accept a coating of tin-glaze. Sprinkle the powder into a pint of water, stir, and brush through a fine sieve. The mixture should have a cream consistency, and more powder glaze should be added if the glaze is too thin. If you wish to check the glaze, as the advanced potter would, it should have a pint weight when mixed of 32 to 34 ounces (about 9.1 kg).

Dab on the white glaze with a large hog-hair brush, and allow it to dry.

Preparation of cobalt oxide or blue stain

A very small spoon (such as a mustard spoon) is required to measure out the cobalt oxide stain. Mix a very small quantity with hot water, and pass through a 120's sieve. A cup-sieve is very useful for this because when mixing small amounts the sieve can rest on an old cup and the liquid is easily brushed through. Now add a small amount of transparent glaze to the stain. You will probably have some ready mixed, and it should be made a little thinner than is necessary when dipping. Since you already have a fairly thick coating of tin glaze on the model the added transparent glaze is really a carrier for the stain. Add the thin glaze until the colour changes to a darkish grey, but lighter than a charcoal grey. Paint areas of the blue stain inside and outside the pot leaving areas to be covered by the green copper oxide stain.

Copper oxide or green stain

Mix this stain in the same way as you mixed the cobalt, but add a slightly larger quantity. When adding the transparent glaze the colour should again be grey, but a lighter shade than the blue glaze. Now fill in the white areas again using a dabbing action with your brush until they are covered over. Finally splash a little of your tin glaze inside and on the bottom of the pot. This extra white will pick up the colours underneath and produce areas of lighter blues and greens.

If you have already mixed glazes you will remember that if left only for a few minutes the glaze powder will settle at the bottom of the container, leaving most of the water at the top. Glaze materials are not soluble and must be stirred frequently when painting. Please ensure that the children paint a fairly thick covering of tin

89

glaze before using the stains otherwise they will not produce the brilliant colours required but will appear black where the pot is thinly covered.

STONE WALL POT WITH COLOURED SLIP DECORATION

Materials and equipment

Clay: Staffordshire Red
Coloured slip stains
White slip clay

Rolling pin
Rolling guides
Hog-hair brush
Paper
Scissors
Knife

You should always carry a stock of white clay powder so that you may have mixed ready a supply of white slip clay. The ratio of powder to water is roughly one pint (0.6 litre) of water to one pound (0.5 kg) of clay powder. When these are mixed they must be brushed through a 40's sieve. When the pot is made it should be placed on a board, ready to receive the coloured slips. You should always work with prepared clay stains so that you can check the colour. The staining is very simple. Using cup size containers mix a heaped teaspoon of stain, add hot water to make a thick cream, and then mix it with a cup full of white slip. Pass it through a sieve and check that the colour is the shade you want. Remember the white clay will have an opacifying effect on the colour and you may have to add more of the stain. On the other hand you may find that the colour is too strong and in this case you may add more white liquid clay.

Once all your colours are mixed the pot will be ready to decorate. Pour the white slip into the pot until it covers the base, then pour out the excess. As you do this you must keep a firm hold of the pot or it will slide off the board. If you have filled dispencers with the coloured slips you should now trail lines across the white base. Trail alternate lines of colour, and trail one of the lighter shades on top of a darker colour, so that when you tilt the pot both colours will run together. One last point to remember concerns the amount of stain you add to the slip. Do not exceed the suppliers' recommended amount or this would probably result in the colour appearing rough or even breaking through the thin layer of transparent glaze.

Glazing the pot

When the pot is fired it will be ready for the glost firing, and this means that it must be covered with a transparent glaze so that the colours are visible beneath the glaze. The pot should be slightly porous at this stage so that it will pick up enough liquid glaze to cover the pot adequately. A 1040 °C firing would suit your purpose.

The correct mixture of transparent glaze must be ready, stirred frequently, and in sufficient quantity for the pot to be fully immersed. The pot must be free from dust, and must not be handled with greasy hands. Hold the pot under the glaze for about two seconds and then remove. It would be better to leave the bottom fully glazed, so it must be placed on a stilt when firing. When removing the stilt which may have stuck to the pot, take great care. It is possible that the very sharp, razor-edge pieces are still stuck firmly in the glaze, and these could cause deep cuts. The teacher should remove these with a large file and then grind the marks on a grindstone.

MAKING POTS FROM NATURAL SHAPES

Materials and equipment

Clay: Staffordshire Red or
white clay according to
the decoration desired
Background glaze
Tin glaze
Stained glaze

Rolling pins
Rolling guides
Craft knives

If all your scholars have brought stones to school you should have a selection of pots of all shapes and sizes. If you have followed the illustrated lesson some will have coiled bases, and others will stand on three legs. It would be exciting to try out several types of glaze decoration on your models, and let the children decide which of them is most effective.

Preparation of background glaze, terra cotta pot

In schools where glazes are being used almost every day there comes a time when dried remains are left in the containers. These are kept and stored in the dry condition. Whatever colour or type of glaze is in the containers, the remains are all dropped into one storage bin or bag. The dry powders are roughly mixed and when the background glaze is required it is made from these varied glazes. One never knows what the final colour will be until the firing is finished and the kiln opened. Sometimes a handful of clay powder is added before the glaze is sieved, and this will give the unknown coloured glaze a speckled effect. This is the first example of a background glaze. The biscuit pot should be dipped into this glaze, leaving it in the glaze bucket for two or three seconds. Then spots of tin glaze should be dropped in close proximity to each other, so that they melt and spread forming a mosaic type of pattern. The tin glaze, which matures at a low temperature, is certain to spread so the result could be quite dramatic.

Preparation of coloured background glaze

You may not be in a position to mix the former glaze, so an alternative for the terra cotta decoration will be necessary. The background glaze can be made from a transparent glaze which is stained with a glaze stain or oxide. The biscuit pot is dipped into this stained glaze and the tin glaze is used as before. Without the spotting with the tin glaze the colour would not be visible. In fact it is probable that it would produce a black or metallic finish which would not be very pleasant.

The white pot

If white clay is used to make the natural form pot then there are several ways of producing an interesting decoration. Simply dipping into a stained transparent glaze would be very effective, or using the stained glaze as a background you could again drop spots of tin glaze on the surface.

Another simple but effective decoration can be obtained by mixing a matt glaze. The glazes mentioned so far have all been glossy so it would make a change to vary the surface texture of some of your pots.

The matt glaze is opaque and a small amount of glaze stain added would give a very pleasant pastel shade. The professional potter will tell you that when firing matt glazes the kiln should be cooled slowly. If the kiln is cooled quickly, and most small kilns cool in a relatively short time, it is possible that the matt may become semi-matt but it is doubtful if the children would appreciate this technical difference.

THE LEAF POT

Materials and equipment

Clay: Staffordshire Red
Copper oxide or green stain
Tin glaze

Rolling pins
Rolling guides
Large needles

In Section One, the making of the pot was illustrated and described, and at the same time instructions and recommendations were given for possible decoration. These recommendations referred to the leaf pot made from white or buff clay. Possibly one of the most beautiful glazes used by potters is one which is made from a combination of tin glaze and copper oxide. The two combined produce a startling turquoise glaze which is enhanced when applied to a biscuit-fired terra cotta pot.

The application may be accomplished two ways, and the first would suit the junior potters.

The leaf pot is first painted with a generous layer of tin glaze. A mixture of copper oxide and transparent glaze is prepared in the way described earlier. The colour is then brushed or dabbed on to the tin glaze.

The second method would mean making sufficient Copper oxide-tin glaze in which to dip the pot, and this means ordering fairly large amounts of tin glaze. If you decide to use this method, you will need to mix a heaped teaspoon to a pint (0.6 litre) of glaze. You may have to adjust the amount of copper oxide when you fire your first pots. A good guide is the colour of the mixture when it has passed through the fine sieve. It should be a pale grey shade, so if the mixture is too dark you must add more tin glaze. If you decide to use the second method, you will need to mix a heaped teaspoon to a pint of glaze.

The brown clay contributes to the beauty of this decoration, particularly in the first method where the colour application is not controlled as it is using the dipping method. The dark brown breaks through the tin and copper and the final result is delightful.

FISH TANK ARCHES

Materials and equipment

Clay: Staffordshire Red or white clay

The fish arches or tank rockery require no glaze decoration, and the use of pottery oxides might be dangerous to the health of the fish. If you wish to introduce colour into the arches you could stain the white clay before it is biscuit fired. The modelled plants or sieved clay could be stained with a green clay stain which when fired would be most unlikely to affect the fish.

FUN ANIMALS: SEALS

Materials and equipment
Clay: Staffordshire Red   Knife; modelling tool

The seals are decorated with the cobalt and copper glazes. These colours give the effect of water on the seal's back when the cobalt blue is dabbed on to the tin glaze. They can be made from white clay and dipped into a transparent glaze which has been stained with iron oxide, or of course they may be coloured with pottery crayons or painted with underglaze colour.

For any of the figures you may make, whether fun animals or characters, you have the choice of using white clay, and using special paints or crayons for your decoration. If you use the Staffordshire Red clay, a covering of glaze is all that is necessary. If you can obtain a bronze coloured glaze from your experiments this would make an attractive covering for your modelled figures. One way in which you might achieve this is by mixing copper oxide fairly generously with a matt glaze (Zircon for choice) and then adding a sprinkling of Rutile. Rutile is a brown, fine sand which gives a speckled effect to glazes, and has been used for many years in the decoration of fireplace tiles.

FIRST MODELS

Materials and equipment
Any type of clay

Like most young children, Sarah who is three and a half years of age loves the feel of clay. She presses shapes and makes faces and loves to press the clay into tall shapes which would be the envy of some abstract artists. She paints her pots with coloured glazes, and is very keen to be present when the kiln is opened. The first pots she made and which were fired were made by pressing a piece of clay into her hand. A small piece of white clay is rolled into a ball just large enough to fit snugly into Sarah's small hand. She must be helped to press the clay so that her fingers show the indents made in the clay. She sticks her thumb into the side of the clay and the result is a pleasant little shape. When she has a collection in the biscuit stage she is allowed to paint them with a selection of coloured glazes. She has used green, blue, the new red and gold glazes, and a matt white coloured with a green clay stain. This type of modelling has been used in my work with spastic children. It has given pleasure to many handicapped children whose hands were not in sufficient control, or not strong enough to model the clay without help.

TILES

Materials and equipment

Clay: Terra cotta or white clay

Tile cutters or knives and rulers or paper templates

For most tile decoration white clay will be required. The small square tiles which you see Andrew making are quickly and easily decorated by dipping them into coloured glazes. The glaze should be stirred constantly so that water is not allowed to come to the surface of the dish. The base of the tile must be wiped clean of glaze so that it may be placed straight on to the kiln bat. Separate the tiles so that there is no danger of them sticking.

The children would enjoy preparing twenty or thirty tiles with which to make a table mat or tea-pot stand. A group of children might work together to make a small table for the school. There is no limit to the models the children could make and the making and decorating of tiles should present no problems.

COIL POTS

Materials and equipment

Clay: Staffordshire Red, for preference

Rolling pins and guides
Tile cutters or templates and knives

If the coil pots are made from Staffordshire Red clay the tin glaze decoration is probably the most attractive. The pot which shows incise decoration when fired to biscuit should be dipped in tin glaze, then the prominent clay markings left by the modelling tool should be rubbed lightly with the fingers to remove some of the glaze. Using a glaze stain or oxide, paint each depression made by the sealing mark. Alternatively, fire after the stage where the glaze is rubbed off. This is an extremely attractive decoration.

White clay may be used for making coil pots but it presents problems. There is a tendency for the clay to dry quickly and the coils are apt to crack. The grogged clay is excellent for making coil pots. It fires to a buff colour and could be glaze decorated or, as shown in the illustration, coloured slips could be used to trail down the side of the pot.

THE RABBIT FAMILY (Models made by Mrs. Bellamy, shown on cover)

These charming models were made and given to me by a friend who specialises in making pottery miniatures, and selling them to raise money for special charities. The modelling is simple but extremely effective, and is the sort which young children might attempt. Obviously they will not have the skill which the modeller has, but the style of modelling precludes the danger of figures with arms and legs missing. The decoration is by underglaze painting. This again has been kept simple. The painting is mainly by line and dots, with no large areas of flat wash which is difficult to obtain with underglaze colours.

3 Mixing and using glaze

Transparent glaze

The original concept of a transparent glaze was that it should show the coloured decoration on the pot through the layer of glaze. The modern transparent glaze does this most effectively. Without the glaze none of the pottery colours would develop into the strong and beautiful colours we are accustomed to associate with pottery decoration. Its function in school pottery is to give a pot a glossy finish, and to mirror the slip colours or the underglaze paints beneath the surface of the glaze. Whatever the shape of a pot, however beautiful that shape might be, the pot can be ruined if the glazing is faulty. So it is necessary that teachers understand some of the techniques of glaze mixing.

When ordering glazes of any kind the catalogue will give a classification of 'L' or 'L S'. The 'L' signifies that the glaze does not contain lead. The 'L S' classification means that the glaze contains lead of low solubility. One does not hear of lead poisoning in the industry now, and that is because of the low solubility of the lead in the glaze. Commonsense precautions as outlined in the notes at the end of the book will protect the children adequately. The lead glaze gives good transparency and a very glossy finish to the pot. Some schools prefer to use leadless glazes which are only fractionally inferior. This statement is arguable, for sometimes it is impossible to tell which glaze has been used on a pot.

All the companies supplying glazes to schools recommend ratios of water to glaze powder. These quantities are governed by the biscuit firing temperature. If the pot is highly fired, the glaze will need to be thick so that it will adhere to the pot. If the pot is low fired, and consequently very porous, then the glaze must be thinner, so extra water is added. Many schools whose pottery is fired rather lower at the biscuit stage compensate by mixing a thin glaze which is taken up and covers the pot completely, then fire the glost ware at a higher temperature. Only practice will make you conversant with the porosity of the pot, and the pint (0.6 litre) weight of the glaze required to glaze the pot properly.

Mixing the glaze

Start with 3 lb (1.4 kg) or 4 lb (1.8 kg) of glaze, and add one pint (0.6 litre) of water for each pound. Stir well and pass through a fine sieve (120's). This will make a very thin liquid, but when left overnight to settle you will find in the morning that the glaze powder has fallen to the bottom of the bucket, and the water is clearly visible at the top. You should now decant some of the water until you think the glaze is correctly proportioned. If you decant too much of the water, it does not matter for this can be added again until the mixture is right.

When you dip a pot to sample the thickness, scrape your thumb across the glaze to reveal the thickness, which should be that of newspaper. This is a good rule to follow, and it is a good idea to have some article in the kiln which could be used for sample dipping. My recommendation is that you have a supply of small tiles of all types of clay, and put one or two in every firing to act as samples until you have mastered the art of glaze mixing.

Underglaze crayons

These crayons are made from underglaze colour, and may be used exactly as children use pastel crayons. They are possibly more brittle than ordinary crayons so should be used with special care to prevent them breaking.

The colours are not easily recognised and it would be useful to use a biscuit tile for trials. Simply mark a small area with each colour, and use a number or a code on both the tile and the paper cover on the crayon. Then cover the tile with transparent glaze, and fire. This colour code on the tile will always be available to check any new batch of crayons. The black and white photographs do not give a good indication of the effect of the crayon, but experience shows that the line design or drawing is the easiest method for achieving success, although two of the tiles with the patchwork pattern which Andrew drew on his tiles have fired remarkably well, and have a lovely colour contrast as well as a good covering.

The secret of success is to fire the white clay lower than is usually recommended, have a very smooth texture on the biscuit ware, and dip in a fairly thin glaze mixing. Being low-fired, the biscuit ware will be very porous, and will accept enough of the thinner glaze to give an adequate finish. The pot should only remain in the glaze for a couple of seconds and should be held in the same position until the glaze has dried.

Underglaze (U/G) painting

Some junior schools where pottery has become established, paint with U/G colours quite successfully. There are no difficulties in mixing the colours, but some problems arise when applying it. If an attempt is to be made, then it would be wise to choose flat tiles or slab pottery on which to practise.

When mixing colours, specialists in this sort of decoration place a little mound of colour on to a specially ground glass plate. These are available but not necessary for beginners. The alternative is a large glazed bathroom tile. Mixing-medium can be obtained from your pottery dealer or you can mix a little gum arabic powder with warm water and this will serve just as well. Using an old table knife or palette knife, mix and grind the powder with a little of the liquid until it is a creamy blob on the tile, then add a little water to make the colour the consistency of ordinary school paints.

When applying the colour, always be economical, for a very little colour will cover a large area. Your tile will probably be quite porous, and you can best test this by touching the biscuit fired pot with the tongue before applying any glaze. Whatever the porosity of the pot may be you will have to place it under the tap for a few seconds. If the pot is highly fired then one or two seconds will be long enough. The water in the tile or slab pot helps the underglaze colour to spread and your painted lines to be even.

Precautions: Do *not* attempt a large area of flat-wash, for it will be difficult to obtain an even texture. Do *not* paint several layers of paint on top of each other or the colour will break through the thin glaze covering.

Finally, let the pot dry thoroughly before dipping it into the transparent glaze. When dipping, have enough glaze mixed so that the pot is completely covered. Leave in the glaze bucket only a few seconds, remove, and retain in your hand until the glaze has dried. Where the fingers have prevented the glaze coming into contact there will be bare areas. Just touch these with a brush full of glaze and the pot is then ready for firing. Do remember, if there is glaze on the bottom of the pot it must be cleaned off, or the pot must be placed on a stilt.

4 Firing a new kiln

Makers of electric pottery kilns recommend a first firing of kiln and kiln shelves at approx 900 °C. There should be no pots in the kiln when the strength of the shelves is being tested. Shelves are often referred to as bats, and the supports used to build up the bats are known as props. Another recommendation is that the bats should be painted with a 'bat wash'. This helps to prevent glazed pots from adhering to the bat if excess glaze has been left on the foot. Flint powder may be used as an alternative, but neither of these materials will prevent glaze from flowing due to over-firing, or if you have glazed your pot too thickly. Thick layers of glaze will run and bead on the bottom of the pot, and could drop on to the bat below.

When you have made your first pots, allow them to dry out thoroughly. If you can rub your finger on the pot and remove clay in powder form then they are 'powder dry' and ready for their first firing. Fill the kiln to capacity if you can, and providing the pots are sufficiently strong they may be piled up inside the kiln to fill up all the spaces.

When reading the firing cycle chart supplied by the manufacturer bear in mind that a kiln half empty will reach maturing temperature more quickly than a fully stacked kiln.

Firing

It is sometimes inconvenient to have the biscuit firing during the hours of a school day, unless there is someone whom you can trust to switch off during the early evening. With this, there is the hazard of switching off being forgotten when the kiln would be seriously damaged. Dry clay pots must have a longer firing than glazed pots which are having their second firing. There is a latent water content present in the clay which must be allowed to escape before the kiln is turned to the high position, and this can take several hours. In a normal day you would switch on the kiln; turn the switch to low; allow two hours before turning it to medium; and finally turn to the high position. The full firing to a 1000 °C or over would then take about six hours so this would be a total time of ten hours when we include the two hours on medium.

It is possible that these times are longer than some potters take but it is better to be cautious at the beginning.

Overnight firing

A safe method of firing is used by many school potters which precludes risks of any kind. The switch is placed on the low setting at 4 o-clock, or whenever the teacher leaves; it is left in this position overnight, and the following morning the setting is immediately turned to high. The long firing at the low temperature allows all the water vapour to escape, and the pots are ready for full heat. Some teachers use the medium switch for half an hour or so, but it is not absolutely necessary. As mentioned earlier, a small kiln will reach maturing temperature in six hours, and this means that the full firing is completed within the school day. Leave the ventilator brick out, and only replace after an hour of full firing. Imprisoned water vapour is harmful to the elements and in time corrodes the metal parts of the kiln, therefore the long overnight heating of the kiln is allowing the vapour to escape slowly and the kiln will benefit from this.

Glaze firing

When biscuit ware is covered with glaze and placed in the kiln for its final firing it is known in the trade as 'Glost Firing'. Since 'glaze is glass', or behaves in the same way as glass when subjected to great heat, it will be obvious that to protect your kiln shelves, and to protect glazed pots from sticking together that certain commonsense precautions must be taken:

1 Clean off the glaze from the bottom of the pot by wiping. Use thick wet felt.
2 Alternatively, use melted wax to cover the foot of the pot before dipping. The wax will resist the liquid glaze and will burn away in the firing.
3 If you wish the foot to have a coating of glaze to prevent scratching furniture, first ensure that the glaze covering is not too thick, and place the pot on a stilt.

Please remember the warning in the earlier pages about stilts. Sharp points left imbedded in the glaze must be fettled off or ground, and children should not be allowed to handle these pots until this has been done. The pots must be placed separately when stacking the kiln, leaving a space of one tenth of an inch (0.25 cm) between. This means that your kiln space will be limited, and you should make full use of your bats and props to build up to the top of the kiln.

Another point to remember if *only* glazed ware is being fired, is that there will be no long period of low firing necessary, and the whole firing operation need only take six to seven hours. Put the switch to low for half an hour, then to medium for the same time, and then place in the high position.

If you have any other form of heat regulator, and of course there are several, then you should follow out the same procedure by setting the regulator at the recommended positions for low, medium, and high.

Once-fired clay

Some clay merchants supply what is known as 'once-fired clay'. It is possible to model the clay, allow it to dry, decorate the model with underglaze colours, dip in transparent glaze and then fire it. It is also possible to make a pot, dry it out thoroughly, dip in coloured glaze and fire. There are hazards, of course. The pot must not be too thick, for if a thick glazed pot exploded, pieces of glazed pottery would stick to every pot in the vicinity. However, this method of making pots is quite practical, and saves a second firing. The clay needs to be well wedged, and the model should be made from thin clay. When firing, you must observe the rules for firing raw clay so that you do not risk the danger of explosions.

98

5 Adapting the classroom for starting pottery activities

Junior school teachers are lucky if they have the use of a specialist craft-room. When pottery is taught in the classroom, there will be problems of storage and working surfaces. If single or dual desks are to be used it would help if wooden modelling boards could be provided. These should be placed on a double layer of newspaper. Because of the small amount of room available on the desk it would be wise to collect wide, shallow jars for holding water and slip.

Clay which has already been used and consigned to the bin must be wedged thoroughly before starting to model. It could be wedged on the classroom floor on which pieces of sugar paper have been spread.

Collect all the screw top jars you can—and here the junior children will probably excel themselves for they always respond to a plea for materials. Use the lidded jars for dry materials and label them so that the colours and glazes are immediately recognised. Unless you are anticipating using large quantities of glaze, the 14 lb (6.4 kg) packets would be easy to store. You will need shelves and these should be slatted so that your pots may dry safely. In fact you should find all the cupboard and shelf space you can for storage purposes.

Rolling pins take up a lot of space, and have a habit of tumbling out of a cupboard when children open them, so it is a good idea to ask a handyman to put up two brackets, fasten them to a wall or cupboard end, and place the sticks and rolling pins across the brackets (see illustration 119 on the next page).

If your kiln is sited in your stock room, and so near at hand, it will be convenient for constant checking of the temperature. However, if it is some distance from the classroom it will be necessary to keep a strict check on the time the kiln is switched on. Make a note in a special book of the commencement of the firing, and mark down the times when you need to make your readings. Keep a record of all your early firings, making notes of times and temperatures, and use the book also for records of glaze and colour mixings so that you may repeat any which have been particularly successful.

If you have the usual classroom furniture, and even though space is limited, try to procure a woodwork bench. There are countless uses to which it may be put. You will soon discover that a bench vice is useful, and many other tasks will crop up where the bench and some simple tools will help you in your pottery activities. If using plaster-of-paris, let the children scrape the left over plaster on to a piece of scrap paper so that only the very minimum finds its way down the sink. Remember that plaster sets very quicky whether in a plaster mould or in the sink.

You will decide whether the whole class or only a small group will practise pottery during a craft lesson. Experienced teachers will not need reminding of the preparation time required, or the time required at the end of the lesson for clearing away tools and materials, and for cleaning the desks. Clay on the floor can cause a lot of work for cleaning staffs, and the children should be encouraged to take extra care, and make a general inspection of the floor before leaving.

There will be excitement if children are using clay for the first time, and sheer wonder when successful pots emerge from the kiln. It would be worth while after the early firings, when almost everything the children make is fired and decorated to insist on quality. They will soon appreciate that some of their work is not worth room in the kiln, and this will make them try harder to achieve success. Group work is valuable and could provide some interesting work for school decor.

If you have a modern classroom with a pottery area, your troubles will be few, but it will still be necessary to train the students to clean messy boards and equipment and keep the room clean and tidy for all their other activities.

Anyone starting pottery in a specialist room for the first time could contact the author for a copy of the school pottery plan, and should a head teacher have pre-knowledge of such a room at the time of building it would be invaluable to incorporate plans for drains and sinks, and storage space at such an early stage.

119   Brackets to hold your rolling pins.

6 Materials and equipment

If you have a small kiln and are ready to order your pottery requisites then you should start with the following:

Clay: various types.
Glaze: transparent and opaque; coloured glazes.
Clay powder: white and brown in small quantities for making slips.
Rolling pins.
Rolling guides: you might make these from wood supplied by a timber merchant.
Underglaze crayons: for drawing on white biscuit ware, later to be covered with a transparent glaze.
Slip stains: these are coloured stains in powder form to add to your white slip.
Glaze stains: these are stains for colouring your glazes.
Tile cutters: large and small square shapes, and a round shape for cutting clay discs.
Boxwood modelling tools: various shapes.
Paint brushes: these you will have already. Hog hair brushes will serve very well for most of your glaze painting.
Brass wire: for cutting clay.
Modelling boards: these will help you to keep the school desks clean, which must be ready for the following lesson. Of course, a layer of newspaper first laid over the desk top would help to prevent stains on the wood.
Slip trailer: the best type for young people is the 'Polythene dispenser' which has a four ounce (113 gm) capacity, and a screw top nozzle which is easy to clean.
Seger cones: ask your dealer for cones to suit the temperature at which you intend to fire the kiln.
Sponges: the modern cheap synthetic sponge will be ideal.
Polythene bowls, buckets and jugs.
Clay bins: the best are galvanised metal bins which are usually provided for school use.

These are the essentials, but you will quickly discover that there are all sorts of objects which the children can provide which will be extremely useful such as screw top jars, large and small for storing colours and liquid slips. Remember, when you empty a packet of colour into a jar, the jar must be labelled immediately. Try to get a supply of large, wide topped glass jars, which will act as storage jars. With large junior classes and the small amount of time for actual work, it saves time and confusion if such materials are prepared and ready for use. Old table knives are often available and will save the expense of buying pallette knives. The school canteen will be only too pleased to let you have large jam tins which are excellent for mixing glazes and slips. If the kitchen will part with those lovely large pickle jars then they will store your liquid slips and glazes adequately.
You will find that the pottery suppliers are your best friends, and if you choose one who advertises a technical service then you will get lots of help with any pottery problems.

7 Reference tables: the use of clay, glaze and colour

CLAY

Staffordshire Red

FIRING TEMP.   1000 °C to 1100 °C. Becomes vitreous at 1200 °C.

FIRED COLOUR   Terra cotta at 1000 °C becoming darker and less porous as temperature rises.

DECORATION   Can be decorated with white or coloured slips; dipped or brushed with tin-glaze, then stains or oxides applied; incise and relief decoration especially when making tiles, then dipped in opaque white glaze to which rutile has been added.

White or ivory clay

FIRING TEMP.   1060 °C to 1160 °C. Smooth textured clay suitable for modelling, and tile making, or for any type of slab pottery.

FIRED COLOUR   Ivory. The biscuit firing produces drawing paper texture which is ideal for painted or crayoned decoration (underglaze colours).

DECORATION   Excellent clay for any type of pottery decoration. May be made into coloured clay by staining with clay stains; glazed with a transparent glaze and on/glaze paints applied; in the clay state may be covered with coloured slips; in the biscuit stage may be decorated with coloured glazes.

Grogged clay

FIRED TEMP.   1100 °C to 1180 °C. Will fire to 1300 °C before becoming vitreous. Recommended school firing 1080 °C to 1100 °C.

FIRED COLOUR   Speckled buff. The sand acting as a grogging agent is responsible for the speckled effect.

DECORATION   Coloured slip in the clay stage, also relief and incise modelling. Coloured glaze decoration. Especially suitable for covering with white or coloured matt glazes.

Transparent glaze 'L.S.'

MATURING TEMPERATURE	1000 °C to 1060 °C. Brilliant glaze with excellent colour response.
INFORMATION	Will give high gloss transparent finish over any clay. May be stained with oxides or glaze stains. This glaze contains lead but is quite safe to use. If fired too highly glaze will run, but should not be fired less than 1000 °C. The letters 'L.S.' denote 'Low Lead Solubility' (See Health Precautions, Chapter 8).

Transparent glaze 'L'

MATURING TEMPERATURE	1040 °C to 1050 °C.
INFORMATION	A similar glaze to the 'L.S.' but leadless. Produces a finish which is only slightly less glossy than the lead glaze. This glaze may be stained and will respond to any kind of glaze decoration.

Opacified glazes. Tin glaze 'L.S.'

MATURING TEMPERATURE	1000 °C to 1040 °C.
INFORMATION	Tin oxide is expensive and therefore a glaze containing tin is not cheap. It is considered the best of the high glass opacified glazes, and has been used to decorate some of the pots shown in the photographs. It may be stained to give pastel shades. When copper is used to stain the glaze it produces a delightful turquoise. Any relief decoration on Staffordshire Red clay will be enhanced if dipped in tin glaze.

Matt glazes

There are many opacified matt glazes, and a choice may be made from glazes opacified with tin, zinc, titania or zircon. Zircon is a relatively new opacifier, and costs much less than the others mentioned.

COLOUR

Underglaze and on/glaze colours

Before it is fired clay can be decorated with coloured slips. When fired it may be painted or crayoned with underglaze colours and then covered with a transparent glaze and fired again, thereby sealing the colours beneath the glaze. A pot fired to the biscuit stage (first firing) may be glazed and fired a second time, then on/glaze enamels may be used to paint on the glossy or matt glaze and fired for the third time. This firing is known as an on/glaze firing, and the temperature is taken to approximately 750 °C.

Oxides

Oxides are oxidised minerals, and in the raw state do not give an indication of their final firing colours. The experienced potter will use oxide colourants because he has learned the strength of oxide required to stain glazes or clay. Most young potters or beginners use prepared colours. These are made from an oxide base but when mixed with water most of them give an indication of their colour. The main colourants used in schools are prepared from cobalt which produces a large range of blues. Copper is used for greens and turquoise. Iron gives yellows and browns of various shades. Manganese will make browns of many shades, and black.

The range of pottery colours

Underglaze colour	Mixed with water and gum arabic and painted on biscuit ware.
Underglaze crayon	Underglaze colour in the form of a crayon.
On/glaze enamels	For decorating on top of the glaze and firing to low temperature.
Clay stains	For staining liquid for slip decoration.
Glaze stains	Add these stains to glazes, either transparent or opaque.
Coloured glazes	There is a very large range of glazes which are already stained and ready for use. Any supplier will give you a list and indicate the firing colour.
Oxides	These are the raw colours, and are usually only used by potters with some experience.

8 Health precautions

In accordance with the requirements of a memorandum issued by the Department of Education and Science it is emphasised that care should be taken in the handling of all ceramic and enamel colours, due to the presence of small amounts of lead, chromium, antimony, etc, which are potentially poisonous.

Whilst many colours are quite harmless the majority contain one or more of metal compounds which can be regarded as toxic. It is recommended that reasonable care be taken in handling all colours and that strict attention be paid to personal hygiene.

The following precautions are recommended:

(a) Do not introduce ceramic colours into the mouth. Do not smoke or consume food while using the colours.
(b) Do not use colour in dust condition or where there are strong draughts.
(c) Handle the colours carefully, and store in closed containers.
(d) Use suitable protective clothing.
(e) Wash hands thoroughly after using the colours.

Author's note

Copper oxide. This ceramic colourant is used by almost every potter to produce the variety of greens used to decorate pottery. It is important that the inside of a pot used for drinking should not be decorated with copper oxide. It has been established that certain fruit drinks left in such pots can affect the copper to such an extent that it could be poisonous.

Lead glazes. There are no longer serious dangers concerned with the use of lead glazes. However, instructions as to precautions sent out by County Authorities usually point out that in the case of drinking vessels lead glazes should be fired not lower than 1000 °C.

Glossary

Bats	Fireclay shelves for kiln stacking.
Biscuit	Clay which has been fired and is unglazed.
Bottle kiln	Tall bottle-shaped kiln. Fired with coal, and used extensively before the introduction of gas, oil, and electricity.
Cobalt	An oxide used for staining slip clays and glazes. Produces a strong blue.
Coloured glazes	Glazes which may be bought coloured and ready for use.
Coloured slip	Liquid clay coloured with a clay stain or oxide.
Copper	An oxide for staining slip clays and glazes. Produces a strong green.
Crayons	Underglaze crayons, for use on white biscuit ware, and covered with a transparent glaze.
Dispensers	Container with a nozzle. Used for spotting glazes or trailing coloured slips.
Extrude	The action of forcing clay through a hole.
Felt	Wet felt used for wiping off the glaze prior to putting a glazed pot in the kiln.
Fettling	Removing the stilt marks from the bottom of a glazed pot.
Flux	Lead or Borax added to glaze mixings to make the glaze flow.
Glaze	A glossy or matt covering on biscuit ware.
Glost	Term used to indicate a firing of glazed ware.
Grog	A powder made from ground biscuit ware which, when added to clay, prevents too much shrinkage and gives the pot added strength.
Grouting	Filling in the spaces between tiles with plaster or grouting powder.
Gum	Gum Arabic. Mixing medium for underglaze paints. Helps the powder to stay on the pot whilst it is being dipped in the glaze bucket.
Incised	Form of decoration or sealing of clay coils.
Iron	Iron oxide, for staining glazes. Produces a range of colour from honey to dark brown.
Leather hard	Traditional name for clay which is hardening, and can be cut like leather with a knife. Modern term 'soap hard' seems a better description.
Mould	Plaster shape for pressing pots.
Opaque	Non-transparent glazes. Can be glossy or matt.
Oxides	Glaze or clay colourants.

Pancaking	Reconstituting small amounts of clay.
Plaster bats	Solid blocks of plaster, used for drying wet clay.
Plasticity	The modelling quality of clay.
Porous	The fired state of biscuit ware which indicates the thickness of the glaze required.
Props	Supports for kiln shelves.
Pug mill	Type of mincing machine for reconstituting clay.
Pyrometer	Temperature indicator attached to a kiln.
Raw clay	Clay in a plastic condition.
Rolling guides	Thin strips of wood. The rolling pin runs along these when rolling slabs of clay. The thickness of the wood determines the thickness of the clay.
Seger cone	Small cone placed in the kiln. A number on the side of the cone indicates at what temperature the cone will bend.
Sieve	Sieve with fine or coarse numbers, from 20's (coarse) to 200's (fine). These numbers indicate the number of holes to the inch.
Slab pottery	Method of making pots from slabs of clay.
Slip clay	Powder clay mixed with water and sieved.
Spy hole	Hole through which a cone may be seen inside the kiln whilst it is firing.
Stains	Prepared colours for staining clay or glaze.
Stilts	Made from fireclay and used to stand glazed ware on, to prevent base of glazed pot sticking to kiln bat.
Textures	Pottery which has been textured either by using a treated rolling pin, or tiles which have a pressed design. The texturing is done whilst the clay is soft.
Thumb pot	Ball of clay into which thumb is pressed to form a pot, sometimes known as 'pinching'.
Tile cutters	Cutters which cut and extrude tile shapes.
Tin oxide	An opacifying agent for glazes. Glaze may be bought with the correct amount of tin added to make an efficient glossy white glaze.
Trailing	Either by glass tube in rubber bag, or by using a special polythene dispenser, trailing lines of coloured slip down the side of a pot, or trailing on to a flat surface to produce a marbled pattern.
Transparent glaze	A glaze which reveals the colours underneath.
Underglaze	Refers to paints which are applied to biscuit ware which is then glazed with a transparent glaze.

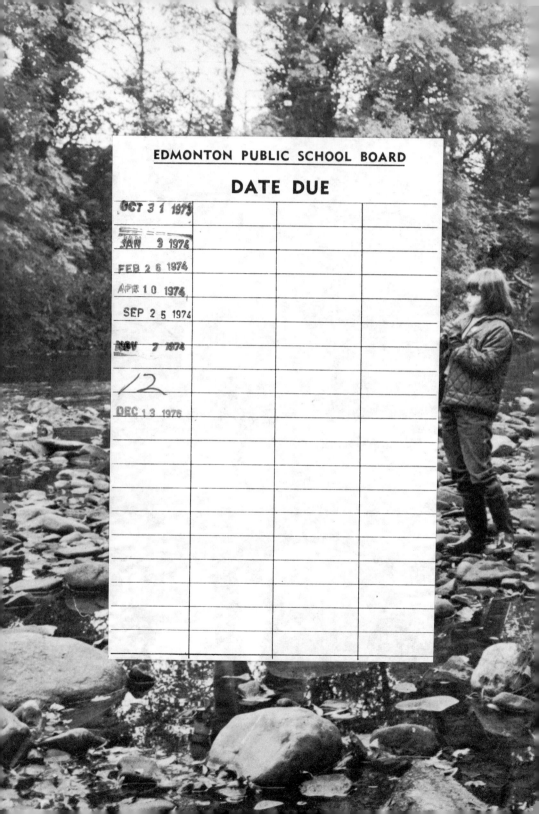